James Pillsbury Lane

Lane families of the Massachusetts Bay Colony

Memorial address at the reunion of descendants and kindred of William

Lane Boston 1651

James Pillsbury Lane

Lane families of the Massachusetts Bay Colony
Memorial address at the reunion of descendants and kindred of William Lane
Boston 1651

ISBN/EAN: 9783337269395

Printed in Europe, USA, Canada, Australia, Japan

Cover: Foto ©Andreas Hilbeck / pixelio.de

More available books at **www.hansebooks.com**

In Memoriam

Lane Families

OF THE

Massachusetts Bay Colony

BY REV. JAMES P. LANE

LANE FAMILIES

OF THE

Massachusetts Bay Colony.

Memorial Address

AT THE

Reunion of Descendants and Kindred

OF

WILLIAM LANE, BOSTON, 1651.

WILLIAM LANE, HAMPTON, 1685.

DEA. JOSHUA LANE, HAMPTON.

WHO WAS KILLED BY LIGHTNING JUNE 14, 1766.

IN THE CONGREGATIONAL CHURCH, HAMPTON, N. H.

WEDNESDAY, SEPT. 1, 1886.

BY REV. JAMES P. LANE.

PRINTED BY REQUEST,

WITH PROGRAMME AND REPORT OF MEETING, "UNSIGNED WILL,
AND OTHER EARLY DOCUMENTS.

Printed by
LANE BROTHERS,
Norton, Mass.

There were other families of the name Lane in New England and the southern colonies in the 17th century. The facts given in this Address and in the appendix to the reprinted "Tear," etc. ("Hampton Lane Family Memorial") are only a part of the material collected and not yet completed for "A Record and Memorial of the Lane Families in America," which has had the attention and labor of the author for many years. The co-operation of all interested in the completion of this work is earnestly desired. and information from any source is gratefully received. The family records of later generations and connections traced to the earlier, and as complete in details as possible are specially desired.

ADDRESS.

The memory of a worthy ancestry and the ties of kindred bring us together to-day in this ancient town of Hampton, where many years ago lived and died the men and women whose virtues we commemorate. In yonder "God's acre," where rest the mortal remains of a number of the heroic and eminent pioneers of our New England civilization, are the graves of our sires and their households. Near them we reverently stand, and over them we purpose to erect an enduring monument to tell coming generations and the world that they live forever. If this our memorial work may prove an example and incentive to others, and lead to the erection of other monuments in that sacred but sadly neglected place of burial, we shall be glad to have thus contributed to perpetuate the names of the great and good who were the crown and glory of old Hampton's colonial days and who ought still to be her pride and boast.

Not among the Pilgrims of 1620, famed in story and in song, nor among their immediate followers in

the growing colony of New Plymouth, but among
the sturdy Puritans who came a few years later and
formed the colony of the Massachusetts Bay, do we
trace our ancestry and kindred, of whom we are not
ashamed, whose character and worth deserve a grateful commemoration.

The Pilgrims and the Puritans were persons of
strong conviction and determined action. The force
which impelled them was primarily a religious force
which entered into all their interests and gave shape
and form, tone and life to all their institutions. The
Pilgrims believed that the national church of England
in its fundamental organization and government as
well as in its forms and practices was contrary to the
word of God, and for conscience sake they took their
stand as Separatists and Independents. The Puritans
did not object in principle to the organization and
government of the national church and desired to
continue in its fold, but they dissented from many of
its rites and observances to which, for conscience sake,
they could not and would not conform. The Pilgrims and Puritans alike aimed at greater purity of
faith and of life, and they alike incurred the enmity
and persecution of those with whom they differed.
The hand of power was upon and against them. And
hundreds of them felt impelled to leave the land of
their nativity to find a refuge and free scope for life
in the land across the sea.

The Pilgrims came first. They were compara-
tively few in numbers, not strong in social position

nor wealth, and the opposition was specially fierce against them. The Puritans were more numerous and embraced many of the highest social standing and wealth who had some degree of toleration. But after the death of James the First and the accession to the throne of his son Charles the First, the opposition was more fierce and the Puritans no less than the Pilgrims were its victims. They too now turned to America for the tranquil and peaceful enjoyment of their rights.

In 1626 Roger Conant and his companions—the remnant of the Dorchester company who three years before located at Cape Ann, but from dissatisfaction with it abandoned the place—removed to "a fruitful neck of land," now Salem. This company of not over fifty persons was the germ of the colony of the Massachusetts Bay, "the sentinels of the Puritans in America." To promote emigration a company of London merchants obtained a patent to "that part of New England lying between three miles to the north of the Merrimac and three miles to the south of the Charles river and of every part thereof in the Massachusetts Bay, and in length between the described breadth from the Atlantic Ocean to the South Sea." During the three years following the first settlement at Salem, accessions from England had increased the number of the colonists to over five hundred.

Hitherto they had been subject to the London company who held the patent, but in 1629, to still further promote emigration, this company relinquished and transferred the charter and government to the colony. Under this stimulus a choice band was organized and in March 1630 a fleet of eleven vessels set sail for the new world. They were for the most part "men of the professional and middle classes, some of them of large landed estates, some zealous clergymen, some shrewd lawyers or scholars from Oxford, some tradesmen. The bulk were God-fearing farmers from Lincolnshire and the eastern counties." Foremost among them, John Winthrop, who was unanimously chosen the first governor of the colony. "Farewell, dear England!" was the cry which burst from the company as its shores from sight faded. "Our hearts," said one to friends left behind, "shall be fountains of tears for your everlasting welfare, when we shall be in our poor cottages in the wilderness." These were men and women driven forth from their fatherland, "not by earthly want, nor by the greed of gold, nor by the lust of adventure, but by the fear of God and the zeal for a godly worship." The voyage was stormy and tempestuous, but on the 8th of July all the vessels were safely moored in the harbor of Salem. Exploring parties went forth to find suitable places for settlement and reported one "up the Mystic," another "about three leagues up the Charles river," another at Charlestown, which they thought would be "a better place for the capital town than Salem." To these places they went to settle, the larger part, including the governor, to Charlestown.

The bright hopes that at first cheered them were soon beclouded by a distressing mortality, occasioned by hardships and a want of nourishing food. Before the close of the year two hundred had passed from the living. The distress at Charlestown was so great that a further dispersion was agreed upon. Some went to Watertown, some to Roxbury, some to New-town, now Cambridge, some to Lynn, some to Mystic, and a few, including Gov. Winthrop, to Shawmut, there laying the foundations of Boston. Over a hundred, disheartened, returned to England. The succeeding winter was very trying. "The wolf of famine was prowling around nearly every door. The governor's last loaf of bread was in the oven, and the prospect before all was death." The 6th of February was appointed a day of fasting and prayer, but was changed into a joyful Thanksgiving, as the day before, the "Lyon" laden with provisions and having twenty-five passengers on board off Nantasket was seen and soon arrived from England.

The tide of trial now turned. Brighter days dawned. The colonists received new accessions from England. The Atlantic was crossed frequently by Puritan emigrants who came to cast their lot with their brethren here. New places were explored and settled. Material resources were increased. The cultivation of the land brought harvests of plenty. Varied industries were developed. A visit to Plymouth by Gov. Winthrop in 1632 tended to unite the two sister colonies in fidelity and love. A just

and honorable policy towards the Indians—taking
nothing from them by force, securing land only by
purchase or free consent—secured their good will and
friendship.   The spiritual interests of the colony were
from the beginning made first in importance.   The
church was organized in every settlement.   It was
as unnatural for them to live without the Sabbath
services and an able Gospel ministry "as for a smith
to work his iron without fire."   The education of
their children was not forgotten.   Schools were provided and the larger part of their taxes were levied
and willingly paid for their support.   And primarily
to raise up an educated ministry and suitable teachers,
with facilities also for other professional callings,
Harvard College was early founded at Newtown, and
the name changed to Cambridge in memory of old
Cambridge in England.

It is a thrilling story, the way the colonial life
prospered and grew, until their very prosperity
brought trials and difficulties seemingly almost insur-
mountable.   Adventurers of no religious convictions,
or of wild superstitious notions inimical to the spirit
and aim of the Puritans, crowded in upon them.
Emissaries of their enemies with subtle guile came in
to subvert their church and destroy their government.
A thousand jealous eyes watched "to pick a hole in
their coats."   A heroic policy seemed to the Puritans
the only one they could have to avert the threatened
danger to the commonwealth, which at such cost and
sacrifice they had planted.   "We came to abide here

and plant the Gospel and people the country; and
herein hath God blessed us," said Winthrop. "If
we be here a corporation, established by free consent,
if the place of our co-habitation be our own, then no
man hath right to come in to us without our consent."
"The intent of the law is to preserve the welfare of
the body, and for this end to have none received into
any fellowship with us who are likely to disturb the
same." Accordingly none were admitted to the freedom of the colony, i. e., to the right of suffrage and
government, but such as were members of some of
the churches of the same. And every person admitted took solemn oath of allegiance, and every male
inhabitant twenty years old and upward, not a freeman,
was sworn to be subject to the government and to
promise obedience to the same. The government
was vested in the Governor, Deputy Governor, and
Assistants who were elected by the freemen. The
substitution of delegates to represent the freemen
was an early proceeding, and in 1634 a House of Representatives to make the laws was established, com-
posed of 24 delegates.

Under this policy was developed a statesmanship
worthy of highest veneration, and a body of laws
worthy of comparison to the famous "Magna Charta."
Under this policy the free pursuits of industry and of
commerce were fostered and protected, the interests
of religion and of education were secured and there
was peace and prosperity to the colony in all depart-
ments of life. Many hardships and privations were

endured which are inseparable from the planting of
institutions in a new country.   To those of an advanced civilization even their prosperity and growth
may seem to have been slow and limited, but to
them they were the occasion of thanksgiving and of
hope for the future.   Side by side with the other
New England colonies the colony of Massachusetts
Bay pursued her way and when she was strongest of
them all entered into a confederacy with them in the
spirit of a hearty fraternity.

That she made some mistakes and committed
some grave errors is doubtless true.   The policy
which joined church and state into one government
or that made the state the servant always of the
church is not what would be tolerated at the present
day.   And it was a happy day for the country when
it was abandoned.   The Pilgrims were in advance of
the Puritans in this and happily their truer ideas of
freedom prevailed.   But in the light of their own
time, we would cover with the mantle of charity
faults and errors, which were prompted by purest
motives, in the times that tried their souls.

We can never cease to venerate the men and
women who "desired to found a new and better
commonwealth beyond the Atlantic, even though it
might require the sale of their hereditary estates and
hazard the inheritance of their children"; "who," in
the words of Bancroft, "were the servants of posterity, the benefactors of succeeding generations";
"who scattered the seminal principles of republican

freedom and national independence ; who enjoyed in anticipation the thought of their extending influence and the fame which their grateful successors would award to their virtues. In the history of the world many pages are devoted to commemorate those who have besieged cities, subdued provinces or overthrown empires. In the eye of reason and of truth a colony is better than a victory." And the colony of the Massachusetts Bay in New England, one of the best, if not the crowning offering in the history of our country.

Among these sturdy Puritans was JOB LANE, who came to Dorchester in 1635 when but a boy 15 years old ; returned to England in 1647 and there married ; came back with his wife and settled in Malden ; after a few years moved to Billerica but later came back to Malden, where he died in 1697. One daughter was born in 1658 and the mother died the following year. He married again in 1660 Hannah Reynor, daughter of the distinguished Rev. John Reynor, first in Plymouth, but afterwards the revered minister of the church in Dover. They had nine children, one son named John and eight daughters. Two daughters died young. The son and the daughters living married well in families that were among the first in the colony, and they and their children maintained a similar standing.

Job Lane and his son John Lane were both men of marked character and influence, identified closely with the colonial government, liberal patrons of the

college and schools, and pillars in the church. The
father was a man of wealth, owning large estate in
Malden and Billerica, and heir to large estate in England, the rents of which he regularly received during
life. He was a carpenter by trade, engaged largely
in building operations, and came into possession of
the Gov. Winthrop farm of 1500 acres, for which he
paid in building a house for its owner, the son and
heir of the Governor. He was very prosperous in
his business. The wealth which he had in the beginning increased to the close of his life. It was
equitably distributed by will to his wife, children,
and grandchildren. The estates in Malden and Billerica continued with his descendants for several generations, and the English estates were not sold out
of the family for more than a hundred years after his
death.

The son John Lane married Susanna Whipple,
daughter of John Whipple, who was one of the first
settlers in Ipswich, a captain in military service, a
member for many years of the General Court, and
the first in this country of a long line of descendants,
many of whom have been distinguished as scholars
and divines, and in various literary and professional
pursuits; a relative also of Rev. Michael Wiggles-
worth of Malden, who was a man of sound learning,
"mighty in the Scriptures," and of the highest social
standing. They had nine children, five sons and four
daughters, seven of whom lived to adult age, married
and had children, the progenitors of a numerous clan

of the Lanes in Billerica, Bedford, Malden, Boston and vicinity and other parts of the country.

JAMES LANE, a brother of Job Lane, came to Malden before 1660 and not long after settled at Falmouth (now Portland), Me., on "Casco Bay, on the east side of Cousin's river in Freeport." From this the point and island near it were called by his name. He was a turner by trade and on first coming to Malden was in the employ of his brother. His wife and two children probably came with him from England. In an attack on Falmouth by Indians he was killed, and his family, consisting of four sons with their mother, were driven away. They came to Gloucester. The eldest son, John Lane, born about 1653, afterwards went back to Falmouth, married Dorcas Willis, daughter of John Willis, an early inhabitant of Falmouth, and settled on his father's place. They had seven children born there, four sons and three daughters. On the second destruction of Falmouth by Indians, he took his family back to Gloucester—where his mother and brothers had continued to live when he went to Maine—and settled "on Flatstone Cove." In 1702 he received from the town a common right and two years later a grant of ten acres on the cove to which his name was subsequently attached. Here were born six more children, three sons and three daughters. His brothers appear to have married and settled near him. The children of these families who lived to adult age also settled here. Their descendants are numerous here and in

other places. Many of them have held prominent
rank as citizens. The section of the town where they
originally settled is called Lanesville to this day.
The first victim of the revolutionary war from this
place was a John Lane. For a number of years the
Gloucester Lanes have been largely identified with
the fishery interest, either as owners or commanders
of vessels, engaged in securing marine wealth. It is
said that the name "schooner" was here first given to
a vessel as it was launched, from the exclamation of
a by-stander, "Oh how she scoons!" One of this
clan of "the Lanes" was Fitz H. Lane, a distinguished
marine painter. Another was Ebenezer Lane,
founder of the well-known "Lane Theological Semi-
nary" in Cincinnati, Ohio, over which Dr. Lyman
Beecher at one time presided, and his son-in-law, Dr.
Calvin E. Stowe, who has recently died, was a
Professor. Several years ago I had the honor to
receive from him, though then over 80 years old,
a very interesting letter giving valuable information
respecting his family and pedigree, and much concerning the institution that he founded and his purposes in founding it.

EDWARD LANE, another brother of Job Lane, came
to Malden in 1651 and began business as a merchant.
He had large capital and a good trade, which he soon
removed to Boston, where he continued in business till
his death in 1663. He was unfortunate in his marriage to a daughter of Thomas Dudley, who succeeded
John Winthrop as Governor of the colony. Although

of distinguished family, with the best advantages of culture, of brilliant mental powers and personal beauty, she was not well mated and made the life of her husband one of great trial and sorrow. Her conduct was the occasion of much scandal, while he had the esteem and confidence of those who knew him. They had one son named Edward, of whom we only know the name and date of birth.

Besides these three brothers, Job, James and Edward, there was another brother who settled in Virginia, and another who settled in New Jersey.

Older than these five brothers was WILLIAM LANE of Dorchester, 1635,—without doubt a kinsman and probably an uncle. It is probable that his wife died in England, and that he came to be with his adult children, who came with him and were moved by the impulses which that year brought large accessions to the colony. The children, all married, were two sons, ANDREW and GEORGE, and four daughters, wives of THOMAS LINCOLN, NATHANIEL BAKER, and THOMAS RIDER, and MARY LONG, widow of JOSEPH LONG. Mrs. Long, with her two sons Joseph and Thomas, lived with her father in Dorchester, and subsequently married Joseph Farnesworth, a widower with four children, by whom she also had four children. Thomas Rider also settled in Dorchester near his wife's father, and there had sons and daughters. William Lane was a man of some property which, though advanced in life, by frugality and industry, he kept until his death in 1654. His will, dated

28 Feb., 1651, proved6 July 1654, mentions new homestead in Dorchester with outhousing, garden, etc., 24 acres of land besides, and various personal property which was inventoried after his death at £82, 10s., 8d.   Though from his advanced age he took little part in public affairs, he was a "freeman" and evidently had the esteem and confidence of the people.   His son-in-law, Joseph Farnsworth, was not only a freeman, but held important offices in the colonial and town governments.

The sons, ANDREW and GEORGE, and the sons-in-law, THOMAS LINCOLN and NATHANIEL BAKER, were among the original settlers of Hingham, took prominent part in organizing society there, laying the foundations of an orderly, industrious and prosperous community. They all had large families. Their descendants are numerous, not a few of whom live at the present day in Hingham, Abington, Brockton, Norton, Attleboro, Taunton and vicinity.   THOMAS LINCOLN was the paternal ancestor of a large clan, many of whom stood high in popular esteem as ministers, lawyers, jurists, statesmen, at least one a State Governor, and one everywhere known, our revered martyr President, Abraham Lincoln.   The descendants of Andrew and George Lane are an honorable line and many of them of superior worth. One of them was John Lane who settled in Norton, Mass., whose descendants hold an annual re-union in the town where he lived and died many years ago. Of this line was the eminent chief justice of Ohio, the

Hon. Ebenezer Lane, LL.D., who attained a national reputation. Some years before his death he was interested in the genealogies of his kindred, and spent some time in England in search of the ancestral seat, which he thought he found at a place called "Lane Hall" in Norfolk Co., and in the neighboring cemetery found a number of graves of the name. To his son, Dr. Edward S. Lane of Chicago, Ill., I am indebted for much valuable information, and I am glad here to name the fact that, although not of our line of descent, he, for the honor of the name, for admiration of the character of our worthy sire, and for sympathy with our undertaking, sent a contribution to the monument fund.

Another of the Puritans of the Massachusetts Bay Colony was our revered sire, WILLIAM LANE of Boston, 1651. When and whence he came are questions still involved in obscurity, upon which we hope after further research, light may dawn. Traditions are conflicting. One associates him with two brothers, one of whom settled in Gloucester, Mass., and the other in Maine, and all three "cordwainers" by trade. We find no trace of these brothers. Possibly James Lane, brother of Job Lane, who was of Falmouth, Me., was the brother of William Lane and figured in the tradition as two brothers from the double residence of his family at Falmouth and Gloucester, but he was no "cordwainer." Another tradition says that he came from Scotland—a true Scotchman of the John Knox pattern, who said

"Give me Scotland or I die,"—but we find no records that give any light in this direction. Another tradition makes him a kinsman of those previously named, not a brother but a cousin of Job, James and Edward Lane, and a cousin also of Andrew and George Lane and their sisters of Hingham, whose father, William Lane of Dorchester, was own brother of his father in England. Certain shadowy indications give probability though not absolute certainty to this tradition. But whatever may have been his origin we have no doubt he was of good stock, and was himself a worthy citizen of the colony. He was admitted freeman 6 May 1652. He was a "cordwainer" by trade, and industrious in his calling. His wife, Mary ——, probably came with him from England. Their children were Samuel, John, and Mary. The mother died in 1656 and he married Mary Brewer, daughter of Thomas Brewer of Roxbury. Their children were Sarah, William, Elizabeth, and Ebenezer. These names and dates of birth, the death of the first wife, and the marriage of the second wife, with dates of the same, and the date of the freeman's oath are all recorded in the Boston records, but we find no record of deaths or burial. Further research may discover these. In the first volume of Wm. H. Whitmore's "The Graveyards of Boston," devoted to "Copp's Hill Epitaphs,"—the other volumes not yet published—are several epitaphs of the name Lane, but none so early as these.

This Thomas Brewer, father of our mother Mary

Brewer, was of English origin, an early inhabitant of Ipswich, afterward of Roxbury, and finally of Hampton, where he died at the residence of his son-in-law Thomas Webster, called "goodman Brewer." We know not where he was buried, but suppose the place was in yonder "acre." He was the ancestor of a numerous line of the name, among whom have been many distinguished persons.

Of the seven children of William Lane Sr., Samuel, the eldest, settled in Hadley, afterwards removed to Suffield, Conn., had sons and daughters, and died there. We have good record of his wife and her pedigree, and of connections, which is of much interest. We also have much that is authentic, though not as complete as desirable, concerning the family.

John, the second son, we also think, settled or afterwards lived in Conn., but we have found no record of his family. There are many persons of the name Lane in western Mass. and Conn., with ancestors recorded of several generations, running back to perhaps the third or fourth from the first, respecting whom we have information, and suppose that some of them descended from either Samuel or John Lane. But the break of one or more generations left out of the record puts us "all at sea" respecting any certainty of origin. Among the scattered tribes of the supposed descendants of Samuel and John Lane are many persons whose character and worth deserve commemoration.

We have found no record of the other children, except of our own sire, WILLIAM, the third son and fifth child.

He was born in Boston 1659, married 1680 Sarah Webster, daughter of Thomas and Sarah (Brewer) Webster, lived in Boston probably until after the birth of their first child, removed to Hampton and resided near the site where for many years stood the old Academy. He was a tailor by trade, perhaps had a shop, but more likely, according to early customs, went from house to house as called for to make clothes for husbands and fathers and their boys. It was a custom in those early days to call tradesmen to settle, much as ministers were called, and we presume he may have been so called to Hampton. It was also customary to make grants of land to encourage settlement. He had a grant of one acre from the town, which in 1717 he deeded to his son Joshua. It has been said that he had a grant of ten acres on condition that he built on it, but of this there is no record in evidence, and it is probably an error. He lived to be over 90 years old, and died 14 Feb. 1749 at the home of his son Joshua, and was buried in yonder acre by the side of his wife, who at 85 years of age died before him, 6 June 1745. Their graves were marked by stones on which were rudely carved the initials of their names only. But these are sufficient to identify the graves beyond a doubt. For many years only the grave of William Lane was known by the rudely carved "W. L.," but there was a space between this grave and that of his son, Dea. Joshua Lane, wide enough for another grave, where, if this was indeed William Lane's grave, his wife would probably be buried. A little more than a year ago our friend Rev. John W. Lane of North Hadley —who has been the pioneer and persistent, patient worker in bringing forward the monument undertaking—with the aid of others dug around and uprooted a tree that was growing here, and found a stone broken into several pieces, that had been crushed by the tree. On carefully putting these pieces together, they made a stone similar in form to the other, and the letters, before obscure, appeared, "S. L.," the initials of Sarah Lane, the wife of William.

They were undoubtedly persons of excellent character. Both were members of the Second Church in Boston, with which they united in 1681, as the records show. That they were in humble life and moderate circumstances is doubtless true, but they were the peers of the best settlers in Hampton's early days. Writings of their son Joshua show in what esteem and reverence their memory was cherished.

In the record of revered ancestry we cherish the maternal no less than the paternal part. From change of name it is usually more difficult to trace, and sometimes impossible. But the mothers as well as the fathers give the stamp of character and of life to the sons and daughters. In the heredity of mental and spiritual endowment as well as in the "strains of blood," the mothers are often the equals of the

fathers, and not unfrequently the superiors. We are
not ashamed of the name of our revered sire, but we
are proud to associate with it the name of our revered
mother. We are glad to know and record the fact
that with the first William Lane of Boston was Mary
Brewer, of the noble Brewer line ; and with the second William Lane of Hampton was Sarah Webster,
of both the Brewer name and the distinguished Webster line.

Thomas Webster, the father of our Sarah Webster, was born in Ormsby, Norfolk Co., England.
and was baptized 20 Nov. 1631. His father died in
1634. His mother married again, William Godfrey.
In 1638, when about seven years old, he came with
his mother and stepfather to Watertown, near Boston. Not long after they removed to Hampton,
where the father was Deacon of this ancient church.
an eminent citizen, influential in all affairs of the
community, and died and was buried in yonder acre
25 March 1671. The son Thomas Webster, growing
to manhood in the nurture of this Christian home,
married in 1657 Sarah Brewer, the sister of our revered Mary Brewer and daughter of the "goodman
Brewer," for whom she cared in his declining days
and lovingly closed his eyes in death. Our Sarah
Webster was the daughter of this worthy couple, who
lived on the "Drake road," so called, owned a part
of the "small gains," and died and were buried in
yonder acre. He was one of old Hampton's best
citizens, the ancestor of a long and numerous line of

descendants, among whom are not a few of distinguished rank in various callings of life, of whom was the eminent statesman of our country, Hon. Daniel Webster, whose pedigree, traced in unbroken line to this Thomas Webster of Hampton, was published in N. E. Genealogical Register, volume IX., page 159.

William and Sarah (Webster) Lane had seven children, all, except the first, born in Hampton, and all reared here, viz. : John, Sarah, Elizabeth, Abigail, Joshua, Samuel, and Thomas.

JOHN LANE, the eldest, married Mary Libbey of Rye. He was a sailor and while at sea was taken by pirates and kept in captivity seven years. After his release he came home. After a while he went to sea again and never returned. They had one child only, a son named for the father, JOHN. This son grew to manhood, was twice married, and was among the first settlers of "the chestnut country," Chester, N. H. He was a commissioned military officer under Gov. B. Wentworth, and retained the title "Cornet" until his death. His life was long, industrious, and eminently useful. He was the father of a numerous family, and the homestead continued with his descendants for several generations, several of whom have been prominently identified with the history of Chester, Raymond, and vicinity.

The three daughters of William and Sarah (Webster) Lane, SARAH, ELIZABETH, and ABIGAIL, married respectively WILLIAM BERRY, ELIAS CRITCHETT, and JOHN VITTUM, and had sons and daughters, whose

posterity we have not traced. We would be pleased
to receive information in this line.

SAMUEL LANE, the sixth child, had wife Elizabeth,
and lived in Hampton Falls. They had seven children, Abigail, Samuel, Elizabeth, Sarah, Mary, Abigail, and Samuel. The three oldest died on the same
day, 2 Aug. 1735, of malignant throat distemper,
which prevailed in many families and was especially
fatal to children. Sarah married Joseph Sanborn, a
descendant of the third generation from Lieut. John
Sanborn, who in 1685 took the freeman's oath, was
one of the earliest settlers of Hampton and prominently identified with its social and civil affairs. His
descendants for a century lived in old Hampton,
"contributing their full share to the bone and muscle
as well as intelligence and enterprise of the community." He was the first of a numerous line in this
country, among whom are many of distinguished
character and renown. Mary married a Mr. Prescott
and Abigail married another Mr. Prescott. We have
not learned the Christian names of these husbands,
and know nothing of their families. Nor do we know
what became of the youngest son Samuel. We would
be glad to have information to enable us to give due
credit to these branches of William Lane's family.

THOMAS LANE, the seventh and youngest child,
had wife Elizabeth, and lived in Hampton. They
had six children—perhaps others—viz. : Mary, John,
Simon, Sarah, Elizabeth, and Hannah. Mary, the
oldest, died in 1739 and the son John died in 1811.

Simon married Sarah Robie and had two sons and five daughters. The mother and daughters Sarah, Elizabeth, and Hannah were all members of this ancient church.

JOSHUA LANE, our revered sire, the fifth child of William and Sarah (Webster) Lane, married 1717 Bathsheba Robie, daughter of Samuel and Mary Robie, born in Hampton 2 Aug. 1696. They lived in Hampton, on the road to North Hampton, about half a mile from the railway station, and where now resides Reuben L. Seavey, Esq., a lineal descendant. The same year as his marriage he had a deed from his father of the one-acre grant, which was a part of the homestead estate that has continued in the families of lineal descendants to this day. In addition to the care of his farm he carried on the trade of a cordwainer, or shoemaker and tanner, building up a large business and establishing a reputation for the quality of his goods second to none in the county.

They united with this ancient church in Hampton —the oldest church within the present limits of New Hampshire—on the same day in 1718, at which time he drew up and signed the "Act of Consecration," which is still preserved in his handwriting. Though not original with him—it is given in Doddridge's "Rise and Progress"—it was certainly heartily accepted by him and breathed the spirit of a whole-souled piety such as characterized his long and useful life. Though his wife's name is not attached to it, we have no doubt she also heartily accepted it, as

her life was in hearty accord. Not long after, he was
chosen Deacon and held the office, faithfully fulfilling
the trust, until his sudden death.

His funeral was very largely attended. His children and their households, numbering over eighty
persons, besides many from Hampton and vicinity,
came to honor his memory. The funeral address was
by his son, Dea. Jeremiah Lane of Hampton Falls;
subsequently printed under the title, "A Memorial
and Tear of Lamentation." Copies of the original
edition are very rare. But a year ago, by the liber-
ality of Dr. J. W. White of Nashua and others, a re-
print as nearly *fac simile* as possible, with appended
genealogical records, was issued under the title,
"Hampton Lane Family Memorial," and a copy given
to every contributor of one dollar or more to the
Monument Fund.*

His wife had died only a few months before, 13
April 1765. She was a woman of superior intelligence and worth, a help-meet indeed in all the interests and work of his life. She was a lineal descendant
in the third generation from Samuel Robie, who came
to this country as early as 1639 from Yorkshire,
England, where he was born at Castle Dunington,
the family-seat, 12 Feb. 1619. Buried in yonder acre,
near the graves of the revered sire and mother, William and Sarah (Webster) Lane, their graves were

---

*Copies of this re-print are still reserved for the benefit of future contributors
to the fund. A few copies are in the hands of the editor for sale at 50 cents per
copy, at which price it will be mailed to any address on application, or it will be
sent free to contributors of one dollar or more to the Monument Fund.

marked by stones with inscriptions read to this day, identifying, beyond a doubt, the sacred spot.

They had sixteen children. Two died young. Fourteen grew to adult age. Thirteen married and had large families. Every one of the fourteen at an early age became a Christian, and adorned the Christian profession by a life consistent and fruitful in the grace and spirit of sincere piety. To the influence of their early home, the impress of godly parents, the sweet ministries of a helpful, fraternal and sisterly love, we look and find a cause producing such noble specimens of character as these fourteen sons and daughters. And to the word of God, whose promise fails not, to read the assurance verified in their experience in honoring their parents in the Lord, "thy days shall be long in the land which the Lord thy God giveth thee." Families were larger in those days than they are now, but even in those days few were the households of sixteen olive plants around the table, the children of one father and one mother, all nestled in the home shelter. There were pious households in those days as now, but it was rare then as now, for households, *all* of the members to be enrolled as Christian disciples, and every one commanding the confidence, the respect, the love of all who knew them. We would like, if we could, to paint in clear lines and beautiful color before you a perfect picture of that rare Christian home. We would like, if we could, to follow with perfect word painting those princely sons and daughters as they left the dear old home to make new homes, upon which fell the blessings of Providence so like those which fell on the home of their childhood. We would like to tell the story of their children and children's children; of the grand work in life they did; of the honors, not a few of them, attained in some of the highest callings of life; of the lives sublime that many of them lived and, departing, left behind them

"Footprints on the sands of time:
Footprints that perhaps another,
Sailing o'er life's solemn main,
A forlorn and shipwrecked brother,
Seeing may take heart again."

We would like to paint before you our thirteen tribes—one more than of the ancient Israel—as they went forth to possess the land. We quote the written testimony of one—the late Ebenezer Lane, Esq., of Pittsfield—who knew them and who penned his personal recollections of the men fifty years before. In his journal he writes, "I once saw five of them together at my father's house in Stratham. They were truly a patriarchal looking band, neatly clad in the costumes of those times. They were easy in their manners and moderately sociable, not given to loquacity, but talking enough to make conversation agreeable, entertaining and instructive. * * They were all persons of highly respectable character. Eight sons lived to a good old age. They were all mechanics and farmers. Six of them were tanners and shoemakers, one a tailor, and one a carpenter and cabinet maker, and all had farms which they cultivated in connection with their trades. Their work was of the best quality and commanded the highest prices in the market. Their shops adjoined their houses so that they could enter them without going into the open air. None of them were poor, nor were any of them rich, realizing the condition of Agur's prayer. All were men of steady habits, regular and prudent in their intercourse with the world, strictly honest in their dealings, careful in making promises and faithful in keeping them."

We would like to take you to the home of Samuel in Stratham, tell you of his charming wives, the first and second, and of their dutiful 15 children; of his library, the largest and best—save perhaps one—in town; of his thriving business of cordwainer and tanner; of the leisure for study he yet secured, storing his mind for use in public station; of the Christian nurture in his home; of the pillar of strength and beauty he was in the church; and how his townsmen looked up to him as their leader and guide in all civil affairs; of his rambles in the country as public surveyor and the neat plats he made, his campings out at night, with sweet thoughts of the starry heavens above; of his serene old age and triumphant death. Nor would we fail to note the blessed ministry of his better-halves in succession; and the lives of their children, who all rose up to bless the memory of their childhood's home. We would follow them as

they went out, and note their success in life; and
the stars in the galaxy of their posterity; the deacons
and deacons' wives, the ministers and ministers'
wives, the lawyers, the teachers, the doctors, the
statesmen, and wives of such, and others too who in
humbler callings bore an honorable name and made
their mark in the world.   And we would pause for a
moment at the end, to tell of one, still living in a
hoary but vigorous old age, who when a young man
began to write his name with an i—L a *i* n e—and at
length became the first of a line of kindred scattered
in the Empire State and other parts of the country,
and after a long life of faithful service as a Presbyte-
rian minister became the founder and liberal patron
of an Academy in Canisteo, N. Y., which is doing a
grand educational work, and now in the flower of age
writes long soul-stirring letters of heartiest sympathy
with our memorial undertaking and sends a liberal
contribution to our monument fund.

To the homes of MARY and her two husbands and
seven children, from whom descended not a few men
and women of marked character and influence, and
one who, having won degree after degree of honor
from the suffrages of his countrymen, at length graced
the halls of the national Congress.

To the home of WILLIAM in Hampton, his beautiful wife Rachel Ward, and their eight children of
fragrant memory, whose posterity continue in extending lines, in many places having blessed and still
blessing the world.

To the homes of JOSHUA, first in Hampton, afterwards in old Poplin (now Fremont), with his sweet-faced and forceful yet equably-tempered wife, Ruth Batchelder, with their ten children. We would like to tarry here long enough to tell you of his perfect workmanship both as a carpenter and cabinet-maker and on the farm which he made to be the best in town; of the strict integrity of his character; of the genial sympathy and smart housewifery of his wife; and the impress they made on their children; of their famous horse "Jack," who would on no account fail in Sabbath duty to be in his shed at church, even if his master and family for once staid at home, and who on week-days could be trusted alone to haul wood from forest to house, and return alone for another load. We would like to follow these ten children as they went out to found new homes in Candia, Raymond, Deerfield, Epping, Fremont, and Brentwood; to paint before you pictures of these homes, the busy, industrious, and useful lives of their occupants; to tell you of the stations they nobly filled; the generous gifts which some of them gave, and the meritorious works of mercy, of charity, and of Christian education which crowned them for everlasting remembrance; to tell of the men of nobility, the Esquires and town clerks and representatives in the State Legislatures of successive generations; the good deacons; the cultured teachers and preceptors of academies; the ministers of Christ's gospel; the beloved physicians; and those of other calling;

to tell you of the women too, not a few of whom took
rank in beauty and virtue with the foremost in the
land ; of the two sisters who won rank among New
Hampshire poets, whose melodies carry comfort and
cheer to many an admiring friend ; of those who have
won victories as sweetest singers ; of those who as
writers and contributors to the press have an honorable record ; and of those who as faithful wives
proved the helpmeets indeed to husbands who found
high place on the roll of fame—among these one of
remarkable beauty and sweetness of character, who
graced every station she occupied in life till she became the wife of an early schoolmate and friend,
went on with him in their home of cultivated taste, a
prompter and sharer in his honorable ambitions, a
queen in society at home and abroad, giving the halo
of dignity, of wit and wisdom, of sparkle in conversation, as he stepped on and upward in stations of
business enterprise and of civil trust to the Governor's
chair, honored *with him* in name among the highest
in the land, and not unknown in other lands, to whose
loving ministry, and inspiring companionship, crowned
in her departure to heaven, the bereaved husband
gratefully bows, and is pleased in memory of the ancestry and kindred of the beloved and honored wife,
to do a generous and double part in our memorial
undertaking.

To the home of JOHN in Kensington, with his
lovely wife Hannah Dow and their eight children, all
worthy scions of the parent stock, whose posterity in

extending lines take their places in the world and make their mark.

To the home of SARAH in Seabrook, and her husband, the good Dea. Nathaniel Weare, with the five olive plants around their table ; to the homes they went to and the quivers full that God gave them, their posterity extending in no obscure lines.

To the home of the good DEA. JEREMIAH in Hampton Falls, and his sweet wife Mary Sanborn. He whose "Tear" fell so tenderly at his father's funeral. He, the tailor, taking the trade of his grandsire William, yet finding time to use his genius as a penman and artist, producing works of rare beauty, some of which are still preserved ; making gravestones and monuments with inscriptions of rare beauty and taste in arrangement, some of which were in yonder acre and other burial places hereabout. We would like to look upon their seven children and note their progress in this home of refinement and christian nurture ; to follow them as they go from the shade of the home tree ; to trace the lines of their posterity, blossoming and fruiting in beauty and worth.

To the home of the worthy EBENEZER, his bride Huldah Fogg and their seven children. To the home of ABIGAIL and her "goodman" Thomas Berry, and their nine children. To the home of ELIZABETH and her John Robie, lovely and pleasant in their lives, but, so far as we know, unblessed with children. To the home of the youngest son JOSIAH, in the ancestral

homestead in Hampton, with his pleasant and frugal
wife Betsey Perkins and their twelve children; be-
neath whose shelter also lived the maiden daughter
Elizabeth, until she was taken by John Robie to be
the wife and companion of his riper years. And to
the home of ANNE, the youngest daughter, and her
"goodman" Joseph Johnson, who went away into
the woods of Maine and founded a home at Readfield,
blessed with worthy lines of posterity too, as we are
glad to know from recent information, while before
in our ignorance we thought they were childless. In
all these homes we should find a Christian nurture, a
blossoming and a fruiting of virtuous and noble life.
And in the lines of their posterity, had we time to
name them, not a few worthy of special mention and
eulogy.

In all these thirteen tribes were men and women,
brave boys and girls, who faltered not when their
country was in peril; stalwart and true in the early
Indian wars; when the national independence was at
stake in 1776; when England sought to humiliate in
1812; and when the flag of the Union was struck and
trailed in the dust in the terrible years of 1861 to
1865. As a representative of our country's defenders
we hoped to welcome with us to-day the Hon. Samuel
W. Lane of Augusta, Me., the commander-in-chief
of Maine's Army Posts, just returned from their
splendid outing across the continent, in San Francisco.

We are glad and proud that the blood of so noble
and worthy a lineage flows in our veins, and we do

well to hold, as other tribes are doing, our annual or triennial re-unions to strengthen the ties of kindred, and honor the memory of our ancestors. Doubtless among these numerous tribes are some whose character and life are a shame and a disgrace to the name they bear; some whose memory may well rot. And doubtless there are not a few who with many characteristic virtues, have frailties and imperfections over which to spread the mantle of Christian charity. But, all in all, what clans in America can boast a cleaner and better record than ours? While we recall the virtues of sires and mothers, the progenitors of so goodly a stock, and erect an enduring monument over their graves, let us breathe the prayer and strive to be worthy sons and daughters, following on to the end and into the bright hereafter.

PROGRAMME. 11 A. M.

Music.

Address of Welcome.

Rev. John W. Lane, No. Hadley, Mass.

Opening Ode.

Written by Miss Isabella Seavey, Hampton.

With grateful hearts and true,
We gather to review
  Scenes of the past ;
Turn back, O leaf of time!
'Long the ancestral line
Let golden mem'ries shine
  That e'er shall last.

Where leafy branches wave,
Upon our sire's worn grave,
  With silent tread,
We strew fair flowers to-day—
Down the centennial way,
We thankful homage pay
  "Our honored dead."

The freshness of this scene
Shall keep his mem'ry green,
  As time shall wing;
For here we clasp anew
The tie of friendship true,
While sons, and daughters too
  Their tribute bring.

God of our ancient sire,
Wilt thou our hearts inspire
  With thy rich love.
Prepared by thine own hand—
Grant that this favored band
"Meet in the better land"—
  Our home above.

Prayer.

Music.

Memorial Address.   Rev. James P. Lane, Norton, Mass.

Music.

Collation and Social.

Other Addresses.

Report of Monument Committee.

Doxology.

REPORT OF THE MEETING.

The day was one of the brightest and coolest of the season. The church, of which our revered sire was a faithful officer while he lived, freely opened to us their house and vestry. Friends in Hampton and vicinity had made bountiful provision for hospitality. Descendants, kindred and friends, to the number of a hundred or more, came from near and from far. On every hand were cordial greetings and smiling faces. Old friendships were revived, and hands were clasped in fraternal warmth by those who were strangers before.

At a few minutes past 11 a. m., Rev. John W. Lane of North Hadley, Mass., chairman of the monument committee, called to order and in brief, fitting words spoke of the bright auspices of the occasion, and gave to all a cordial welcome. He held in his hand a time-worn book, the original journal of our revered sire, and exhibited other original writings that had come down to us from his time. Among these was the Will which he had written and intended to sign on his birthday which came three days after his death, the "Act of Consecration," signed when he united with the church, and the draft of Constitution of a Young

People's Society of Christian Endeavor, or Young Men's Christian Association, signed by thirty-six young men of Hampton, including Samuel Lane, son of Dea. Joshua Lane. Although this last was not dated, there is evidence that the society was formed not later than 1741 and probably a few years earlier. Other interesting facts of family history were mentioned, the wide-spread and growing interest among the descendants in the monument undertaking, from Maine to Georgia, to California and to the Sandwich Islands beyond, and the awakening of the people of Hampton to a commendable pride in the founders and early settlers of their town.

The opening ode, written by Miss Isabella Seavey of Hampton, a lineal descendant, was sung and prayer was offered by the venerable historian of Hampton, Dea. Joseph Dow, A. M.

After singing "Blest be the tie that binds," the memorial address was given by Rev. James P. Lane of Norton, Mass., occupying about forty-five minutes in the delivery.

After singing "How firm a foundation," an effort was made to ascertain who and how many lineal descendants were present in the different branches of the sons and daughters of Dea. Joshua Lane. This effort was interrupted by the announcement of collation ready in the vestry, to which all were cordially invited.

Grace was said by Rev. James H. Fitts of South Newmarket. The collation was abundant, happily served by the ladies of Hampton and vicinity, and greatly enjoyed, as for an hour or more the flow of conversation, of wit and pleasantry went on. Among the viands was a large ancient pewter platter of

Indian pudding, made by Mrs. Fanny (Drake) Lane of Hampton, who is over 86 years of age, from a recipe used in the family of our revered sire. In her younger days she spent much time in the family of an aunt, the wife of a grandson of Dea. Joshua Lane, who was a son of Dea. Josiah Lane, which families had successively occupied the old homestead. There she became familiar with many of the Lane traditions and customs, and among them this of the pudding. She subsequently married Simeon Lane, a grandson of William Lane, one of Dea. Joshua Lane's sons. The old lady was present at the collation, and on being requested to rise, that she might be seen and known, reluctantly stood up and was received with hearty clapping of hands. Governor Smith offered $5 for the first copy of the recipe from her hand, which offer was accepted, and copies were taken and sold at 10 cents each—all for the Monument Fund.

RECIPE. 1 qt. milk, 1 tea-cup molasses, 4 table spoon-fulls of fine Indian meal, a little salt, 1 tea spoon-full ginger. Boil the milk; stir in the meal while the milk is boiling; add the other ingredients and it is ready for the oven. After it stands in the oven 15 minutes, pour 1 cup of milk over the top and bake slowly, more or less. This was baked in a brick oven.

The water used at the collation for drink was drawn from the old well of Dea. Joshua's at the homestead, and was relished by the company as Jews of old prized the waters of Jacob's well in Palestine.

After collation and social a visit was made to the old burial ground, "God's Acre," and, standing and sitting in a group in the shade of the trees, with the graves of our ancestors in the fore-ground, the company were photographed by S. P. Brown & Co., of Hampton Beach and Lowell, Mass.

Returning to the church at 2 p. m., Rev. James H.
Fitts of South Newmarket was called to the chair.
The effort of the morning to ascertain the numbers
present in the different lines of descent from the sons
and daughters of Dea. Joshua Lane, was completed.
It appeared that there were present sixteen of the
tribe of Samuel, nine of the tribe of Joshua, one of
the tribe of William, fourteen of the tribe of Jeremiah, seven of the tribe of Ebenezer, four of the tribe
of Josiah, and one of Sarah's line.   Others only knew
that they were descendants of our revered sire, but
could not tell to which of the lines they belonged,
tracing only two or three generations, the intermediate
links being unknown, and others were of the kindred
by marriage and in collateral branches.

Alluding to the statement in the memorial address
of the morning that the mothers no less than the
fathers should be cherished, Mr. Fitts said that
it was by his mother that he was of this line of descent.
He then mentioned the way one branch of the family
in Candia remembered the names in the ancestral
line,—two Williams, two Joshuas, two Johns,—and
spoke in tender eulogy of a daughter of the second
John, Emily Lane, the accomplished first wife of
Ex-Gov. Frederick Smyth of Manchester, N. H.,
whose presence to-day is very gratifying to all of us.

The Governor gratefully and tenderly responded,
and spoke of marked characteristics of the Lanes and
Lane families as he had known them from his childhood, of their Christian integrity, their stability, their
reliability in all relations of life, and of the respect
and confidence they inspired in all who knew them.
He commended the memorial address of the morning
and expressed his appreciation of the labor and

research it evinced, and its eloquent and just portrayal of the character of the revered sire and his family. He expressed desire that it be printed and made his generous proposal to meet the cost. He spoke warmly of the monument undertaking and of the prospect of a complete success. Turning to Rev. J. W. Lane of North Hadley, who sat near him, he expressed hearty thanks for what he had done by correspondence and otherwise to originate and carry forward this worthy object. He closed with the impressive lesson which the character of the revered sire and his family, repeated in so many of succeeding generations, so clearly sets forth, of a sincere and eminent piety, crowned with length of days, glory and immortality.

Hon. Martin A. Haynes of Lake Village, M. C. from New Hampshire, was invited to speak and said that he was glad his wife was of this line, though he was not. He expressed great pleasure in being here to-day, had been deeply interested and moved by the memorial address of the morning, and felt grateful to the author for his labor and research and the eloquence of his utterances. Said that he liked the word "clan" as used by the speaker, and made a distinction between the true and noble "clannish" spirit and that which the word sometimes designates. He spoke of the great value of such family re-unions, in promoting the ties of kinship, fostering memory of virtuous ancestors, and giving motive to virtuous and honorable life. He expressed hearty sympathy with the purpose to erect an enduring monument over the graves of our worthy dead, and congratulated the kindred upon the assured success of their undertaking.

Rev. John W. Lane of North Hadley, Mass., spoke

in humorous vein of his connections with this line, not only by his father and mother, but by his step-mother too, both whose grandmothers, Mary Shaw and Abigail Berry, were daughters of Dea. Joshua Lane, claiming that thus he probably had more Lane blood in his veins than any of the rest of us. More seriously he spoke of the interest he had felt for several years in the monument undertaking; tenderly alluded to some words of his father before his death and the purpose they inspired in his own heart; spoke of the joy of an extensive correspondence during the year past in the interest of the monument, of the generous responses received both in encouraging words and substantial contributions, making special mention of Rev. Lewis F. Laine of Canisteo, N. Y., who, though old and deaf and far away, had shown an enthusiastic interest in the work.

Col. John M. Weare of Seabrook spoke of his interest in this meeting, and expressed a wish for a regular annual gathering of the Lanes and allied families, to promote fellowship and strengthen the ties of kindred. He mentioned interesting facts concerning his branch and gave some items from a genealogical record he had prepared for the author of the memorial address.

Brief remarks were made by Levi E. Lane, Esq., of Hampton Falls, George W. Lane, Esq., of Salem, Mass., Dea. Joseph Dow, A. M., of Hampton, John G. Lane, Esq., of Manchester, and others. An interesting letter was read from Timothy O. Norris, A. M., of Troy, Davis Co., Iowa, formerly Principal of Hampton Academy, and a descendant in the line of Joshua, giving reminiscences, expressing interest in the occasion, and regret for necessary absence. Letters of sympathy and regret for necessary absence were mentioned as received from Com. Samuel W. Lane, of Augusta, Me., Edward B. Lane, M. D., of Boston, and others. The absence of Dr. J. W. White, of Nashua, who made the generous proposal last year for re-printing the "Tear," etc., was noticed with regret by many; and regret was deepened on subsequently learning that it was caused by sickness.

The subject of publishing a genealogical record was introduced and discussed, but no definite action was taken. Rev. James P. Lane of Norton, Mass., spoke of the interest he had felt for many years in this matter and of the material he had collected, and expressed a desire to receive from any one and all interested such information as might be useful in completing the work.

The monument committee reported several designs for a monument, one of which they specially approved, to be of Quincy granite. The treasurer reported the amount of the fund, now paid in, to be over $340, and increasing as the kindred became interested. Three days after this meeting a contribution of $25 was received from a descendant in Wisconsin. Up to the time of going to press the fund amounts to $370.60. The prospect of securing the desired $500 is assured. This will probably be sufficient to prepare the ground and erect the monument. Additional contributions will be needed to create a fund for perpetually caring for and preserving the monument. All contributions paid in are on interest till needed for the purposes for which they are given.

On the question of another meeting next year, a general desire for such a meeting was expressed, with the suggestions that notice of it be more widely given and effort made to secure larger attendance, and that at the meeting an organization be effected with a full board of officers and committees for regular re-unions thereafter for fellowship. It was stated that the year 1888 would be the 250th anniversary of Hampton's history, that meantime the monument committee could complete their trust, and the monument be dedicated at a re-union that year, in connection with other commemorative exercises of the town. The calling of the meeting next year was left with the monument committee.

Votes of thanks were passed to the church for the free use of their house and vestry, to the friends in Hampton and vicinity for their generous hospitality, to Mrs. Cornelius Philbrick, of Rye, the organist of the day, for her aid in the service of song, and to Rev. James P. Lane, of Norton, Mass., for his Memorial Address, requesting, in accord with the generous proposal of Gov. Smyth, that it be printed in full. Mr. Lane responded with thanks for the very kind and cordial reception of his effort, his pleasure in being able to contribute to the interest of the occasion, and his assent to their request.

After singing "Praise God from whom all blessings flow," adjourned to meet next year at the call of the monument committee.

What a delightful meeting we have had! was said by many as the company departed their several ways. May this be an omen and sure prophecy of still better and larger meetings in the future.

THE UNSIGNED WILL.

This was written with the evident intention to sign it on his birth-day when he would be 70 years old, but he was killed by lightning three days before. It is carefully preserved in his own hand-writing, and its provisions were doubtless carried out by his children. It is of special interest not only as giving insight to possessions, but also as showing his spirit of piety, his care for the peace, welfare and good name of his children, his wise discrimination in providing a home for the unmarried daughter, and his tender memory of the beloved wife and daughter gone before, in special gifts to the living grand daughters of the same name.

"In the Name of God, amen, the Seventeenth Day of June, anno Domini 1766, I, Joshua Lane of Hampton, in the Province of New Hampshire, Cordwainer, being well and in Bodily Health and of a Sound Disposing mind and memory, thanks be given unto God:

Calling to mind the mortality of my Body, knowing that it is appointed for all men once to Die; Do make and ordain this to be my Last Will and Testament, that is to say, Principally and first of all, I give and Recommend my Soul into the hands of God that gave it; and my body

I Recommend to the Earth, to be Buried in a Christian Decent Burial, at the Discretion of my Executors; nothing Doubting but at the General Resurrection I shall Receive the Same again by the mighty power of God.

And as touching such worldly estate wherewith it hath pleased God to Bless me in this Life, I give Devise and Dispose of the Same as follows, viz.

Imprimis. I give unto my Seven Sons, viz. my Son Samuel Lane, my Son William Lane, my son Joshua Lane, my Son John Lane, my Son Isaiah Lane, my Son Jeremiah Lane, and my Son Ebenezer Lane; and also to my Daughter Anne Johnson, Each five shillings, to be paid within on year after my Decease by my son Josiah.

Item. give unto my three Daughters viz. my Daughter Mary Shaw, my Daughter Sarah Weare and my Daughter Abigail Berry each five shillings, and each of them one of my Feather Beds to be paid and Delivered within one year of my Decease by my Son Josiah.

Item. I give unto my Daughter Elizabeth Lane Twelve Pounds and Ten Shillings Lawful Money to be paid to her within one year after my Decease by my Son Josiah. I also give her one Cow which has usually been called hers; and also that Feather Bed on which I usually Lay; and my Brass Kettle; my largest Iron Pott; my largest Handirons, and one Framel, and my Loom to be delivered to her within three months after my Decease. I also give to my Said Daughter Elizabeth so long as She Lives Single before Marriage, the use of the Northwesterly Corner Chimney room of my Dwelling House; and the small House adjoining to it; and the fore Chamber at the East End of my House, with a privilege in an oven, & cellar & well for her own use, and not to Lett out to any Person; I also give her four Bushels of Indian Corn and one Bushel of English; fourteen Pounds of flour; Sixty Pounds of Pork & thirty Pounds of Beef; two Cords of Wood; and the keeping of one Cow winter & Summer; and the priviledge of a garden, all which is to be found and provided for her yearly During Said Term of her Single Life by my Son Josiah.

Item. I give to my three grand daughters Bathsheba Lane, Daughter of my Son Samuel, and Bathsheba Shaw, Daughter of my daughter Mary, and Bathsheba Johnson, daughter of my Daughter Anne, to each of them and their Heirs, fifteen Shillings Lawful Money apiece to be paid.

Item. I give unto my Son Josiah Lane, His Heirs and assigns forever, (after my Debts and Said Legacies and funeral charges are paid) all the Remainder of my Estate both Real and Personal of all kinds whatsoever and wheresoever the Same is or may be found.

And further my Will is and I do hereby constitute, appoint and ordain my aforesaid Sons Samuel Lane and Josiah Lane to be my Said Executors of this my last Will and Testament———and I do hereby utterly Disallow, Revoke and Disannul all and every other former Testaments Wills and Legacies, Bequests & Executors by me in any ways before this time Willed and Bequested; Ratifying and Confirming this and no other to be my Last Will and Testament. IN WITNESS whereof I do hereunto Set my hand and Seal the Day and year aforementioned.

(L. S.)

Signed, sealed, pronounced and declared by the sd Joshua Lane to be his Last Will and Testament in presence of us the Subscribers.

THE JOURNAL.

This is a time-worn book six inches long, four inches wide, one half inch thick, bound in parchment with a brass clasp and having a pocket to one of its covers. It is closely but plainly written, and covers a period of more than twenty-eight years, from Jan. 14, 1727 to Dec. 27, 1755. We find here personal meditations on various themes and occasions; an account of the deaths in the Parish and Town from 1727 to 1755 inclusive; notice of an earthquake, Oct. 29, 1727, "in which there was much of God's infinite and Almighty power made manifest, and also much of the great mercy of God in sparing a sinful people"; meditations on the sickness and death of his son Josiah, twin of Joshua, who was born July 8, 1724, and died July 22, 1729; notice of the death of other children in 1735 by the "awful throat distemper"; personal reflections on his birth-days, (O. S.) June 5, 1732, '33, '39, '41, '44; additions to the church in Hampton, 1732, '33, '42, '43, '44, '50; etc.

The heart of the man and the beauty of his soul sustained by grace in a sore trial are manifest in his meditations on the sickness and death of his son, Josiah. After a statement of the sickness and the alternation of hope and despair of recovery, until "he fell asleep in Jesus, one of those lambs whom our Lord Jesus Christ would gather in his arms and carry in his Bosom," he continues:

"It was admirable with what patience that child bore up all along under his pain and illness. All the time of his sickness he was seldom known to complain when awake, but when in a drowse or sleep his groans were enough to pierce the stoutest heart; but when he was awake he would seem to look and speak pleasant. He departed this life July 22, 1729, being five years and a fortnight old that day he died at night.

And now God's holy will is done. O that I may so behave myself under my present affliction that God may be glorified by me, and so that I may have occasion to say in the end that it is good for me that I have been afflicted. I know O Lord that Thy judgments are right and that in faithfulness Thou hast afflicted me. Surely it is meet to be said unto God, I will not offend any more. O Lord let my heart be weaned from this world, and the dearest enjoyments of it. And let my heart's delight be in Thyself, and my longing desire after Thee, for Jesus Christ, His sake, Amen.

But surely it becomes me to take great notice of the mercies of God to me. as well as of His afflictive dispensations. Though God was pleased to take one so dear a child from me by death, yet was he pleased in the midst of Judgment to remember mercy, and spared two of my other children. viz., John and Sarah, who were dangerously ill at the same time with the same distemper and brought very low, but yet raised up even from the mouth of the grave. O that I may never forget how good God has been to me, who am altogether unworthy even of the least of His mercies. And O that I might but truly love God, and then all things shall work together for my good.

O Lord my God I will praise Thee. Though Thou wast

wroth with me Thine anger is turned away, and Thou dost comfort me."

His birth-day reflections express gratitude to God for innumerable mercies, a filial recognition of His hand in trials of affliction, humble confession of sin, and earnest prayer "to magnifie Thy rich mercy in pardoning of me and enable me by thy grace for the remainder of my days in all things to walk as becomes a disciple of the Blessed Jesus." On his forty-fifth birth-day he wrote as follows:

"June y⁵ 5th, 1741. God in his great mercy has Returned upon me another Birth Day. I am this Day forty-five years old—and I hope God has made this Day a good Day to my soul—It was one of our private meeting days and it pleased God to incline the ear of our Rev. pastor to preach to us at the house of my Dear Brother Dⁿ Joseph Philbrick's from those precious words of Christ: in Mat. 18, 20. Where two or three are gathered together in my name there am I in the midst of them.

I hope it pleased God to meet my heart in this sermon —Oh may I become united to my Dear Savior by a living faith—that so I may become fruitfull under this Day's and all my precious enjoyments.

Oh that I might from this Day forward keep more close to God than ever I have yet done, and that I may at all times exercise myself to keep a conscience void of offence, both towards God and towards man."

On a separate slip of paper, in his handwriting, and kept in the pocket of this book, apparently that it might be readily consulted and repeated, the following is found, which we have entitled a

PRAYER OF CONSECRATION.

"O that I might always be in the exercise of faith in Jesus Christ, O how sweet would it be and how pure would my heart and my conversation be; as in Acts 15, 9; purifying their hearts by faith, and Gal: 5, 24, and they that are Christ's have crucified the flesh with the affections and lusts: and O that I could but by faith apply God's promises of cleansing my heart and subduing my iniquities as Ezek. 36, 25 then will I sprinkle clean water upon you and ye shall be clean, from all your filthiness will I cleanse you, and also in Mic. 7. 19 He will subdue our iniquities, and 2 Cor. 7. 1 Having therefore these promises—let us cleanse our selves from all filthiness of the flesh and spirit, perfecting holiness in the fear of God—and O that I might have the Blessed Assistance of the Spirit of God; that so I may through the Spirit mortifie the Deeds of the body that I may live. Rom. 8, 13."

THE YOUNG MEN'S SOCIETY.

During the ministry of Rev. Ward Cotton a young men's association was formed, with his cordial sympathy and encouragement. We do not know the date of it, but it was before 1741, at which time Samuel Lane, son of Dea. Joshua Lane, one of its members, moved to Stratham. We presume it was several years before this, for on the 5th of Feb. 1741-2 the society was re-organized, or a second society of similar character was formed under a constitution of fourteen articles, with twenty-three members. The manuscript History of Hampton, by Dea. Joseph Dow, A. M., has a full account of this. We hope the town will take measures to have this valuable work published. That year, 1741-2, there was a great religious awakening in Hampton, as in many other places in New England, and a large number were added to the church. This Young Men's Society was one of the honored agencies of the Holy Spirit in promoting this work of Grace.

Among the papers of Dea. Samuel Lane of Stratham, in his hand-writing as it was in his youth, is a copy, without date, of the original articles of association and thirty-six signatures of the members, as follows :

ARTICLES of the young men's meeting at the Schoolhouse in Hampton.

Those that seek me Early shall Find me. . . . .

We whose names are hereunto Subscribed being Sensible that it is our duty to Glorifie God in the days of our youth: to seek first the kingdom of God and his Righteousness, and to exhort one another dayly; we do for the attaining of these things (with the consent of our Pasture) form ourselves into a society for the worship of God, and that our meetings may be to the edification of our selves & without offence to any others we do oblige our selves to the observance *of these following articles: viz*

1ly We will meet together every Lord's day evening at such houses or house and hours as shall hereafter be agreed upon by us.

2ly We will be constant upon our attendance upon the meetings, and if at any time we are absent, we will be ready to give a reason for it to the society, and will not be offended when the reason is demanded.

3ly Att these meetings we will pray together & then read a sermon or some other book of piety, then conclude with prayer and the singing of a psalm.

4ly At our meetings we will have no worldly discourse: nor speake evil of any.

5ly We will maintain a brotherly love to all the members of the meeting and will at all times treat one another with tenderness and affection.

6ly When we see or hear of any of our society falling into any sin we will in a brotherly manner reprove him for it, and he shall without being offended thankfully except of a reproof.

7ly We will be carefull of one another's reputation. We will not publish any fault we know in one another, and we will be especialy care full not to deride or speak meanly of any for any thing done in the meeting.

8ly When the meeting is done every night we will im-

mediately in a sober and orderly manner retire to our own
Home.

ISRAEL JAMES	Thos NUDD	Benjn JAMES
Samll LEAVITT	JOSEPH JOHNSON	Ebenr SAMBORN
JOHN MOULTON	JOSHUA WINGET	JOHN CRASBIE
SHUBEL PAGE	OBEDIAH MARSTON	Jonan LEAVITT
Wm JANNENS	JOHN SAMBORN	JAMES JOHNSON
JOHN LAMPREY	MATTHIAS TOWLE	AMOS TOWLE
JEREMIAH PAGE	SIMON BACHELDER	Thos ELKINS
ABNER FOGG	DANIEL FOGG	Wm CLEFARD

Thos RAND	JOHN SLEEPER
Jonan FREESE	BENJ SAUTER
JEDEDIAH SLEEPER	JABEZ JAMES
SAMUEL LANE	Jonan SAMBORN
Jereh BACHELDER	Thos WEBSTER
ELISHA TOWLE	JEREMIAH ELKINS

BURIALS IN THE OLD BURIAL GROUND, "GOD'S ACRE."

Of the first settlers of Hampton—says Dr. Jesse Appleton in his Dedication discourse, 14 Nov. 1797—only sixteen had transmitted their names to that time, and only four of these were continued in Hampton. How many of these, and of others whose names had ceased in the town's annals, were buried in the old burial ground we know not, but doubtless the bodies of many of them there rest, whose names and lives are worthy of remembrance. By the changes of time some of these graves are beyond identification and others are passing into the same oblivion. But there are still many that may be identified and should be marked by fitting memorial to ·tell the world of those who once lived and contributed their part in the life and virtue of old Hampton's colonial days. We pray that there be a rallying of the clans interested, to reclaim that "God's Acre" from its sad condition of neglect and to make it beautiful and attractive to present and future generations who may come here and use—in the words of the immortal Webster—"that noble faculty of our nature which enables us to connect our thoughts, our sympathies and our happiness with what is distant in place or time and, looking before and after, to hold communion at once with our ancestors and our posterity."

Five ministers of this ancient church who died in office are buried here. To these we append a list of burials as copied by a friend on a recent visit. Further research would doubtless discover others. Following this list is a cut of the stones at the graves of William and Sarah (Webster) Lane, the one whole as it has stood for 137 years, the other restored from the broken pieces crushed in the tree, as stated in the memorial address.

REV. TIMOTHY DALTON. 1641-1661. Died Dec. 28, 1661. Aged 84 yrs.
REV. SEABORN COTTON. 1660-1686. Died Apr. 19, 1686. Aged 52 yrs.
REV. JOHN COTTON. 1696-1710. Died March 27, 1710. Aged 52 yrs.
REV. NATHANIEL GOOKIN. 1710-1734. Died 1734. Aged 48 yrs.
REV. EBENEZER THAYER. 1766-1792. Died Sept. 6, 1792. Aged 58 yrs.
DEA. PHILEMON DALTON, d.1721, 57 y. PHILEMON DALTON, d.1751, 82 y.
ISABELLA, eldest child of Rev'd Ward and Joanna Cotton, 17 y.
DR. JOHN WEEKS, d. 1763, 47 y. MARTHA, his wife, d. 1758, 40 y.
Son of Jacob Freese, d. 1727, 1 y. SALLY, w. of Joshua Mace, d. 1795, 28 y.
JOHN MOULTON, d. 1794, 45 y. CAPT. JEREMIAH MOULTON, d.1795,38y.
SAMUEL PALMER, d. 1761. MRS. ELIZABETH PALMER, d. 1744.
SAMUEL CHAPMAN, d. 1722, 68 y. JEREMIAH LAMPRE, d. 1762, 23 y.
MOLLY LAMPRE, w. of Reuben Lampre, d. 1772, 22 y.
MIRIAM LAMPREY, w. of Dudley Lamprey, d. 1796, 23 y.
NATHANIEL LAMPRE, d. 1769, 72 y. JOSEPH HOBBS, d. 1717, 25 y.
JONATHAN HOBBS, d. 1715. SARAH HOBBS, w. of Morris Hobbs, d.1717, 66 y.
DOCT. BENJAMIN DOLE, d.1707, 27 y. CAPT. NATHANIEL DRAKE, d.1763, 69 y.
MARY BATCHELDER, D— to Thomas Batchelder.
ABIGAIL PRESCOTT, formerly consort of Deacon—
MRS. DOROTHY SMITH, wife of Major Joseph Smith, d. 1706, 50 y.
MRS. HANNAH, consort to Mr. John Moulton.
MRS. RACHEL, consort to Mr. William Moulton, d. 1774, 80 y.
DEA. JOSIAH MOULTON, d.1776, 90 y. MR. HENRY DEARBORN, d. 1756, 68 y.
MR. JOSIAH MARSTON, d. 1834, 78 y. CAPT. JEREMIAH MARSTON, d, 1803.
SAMUEL TOUIL, son of Caleb and Zeper Touil, d. 1736, 13 y. [d. 1776, 26 y.
MR. JEREMIAH TOWLE, d. 1800, 90 y. MERIBAH FOGG, dt. to Mr. John Fogg,

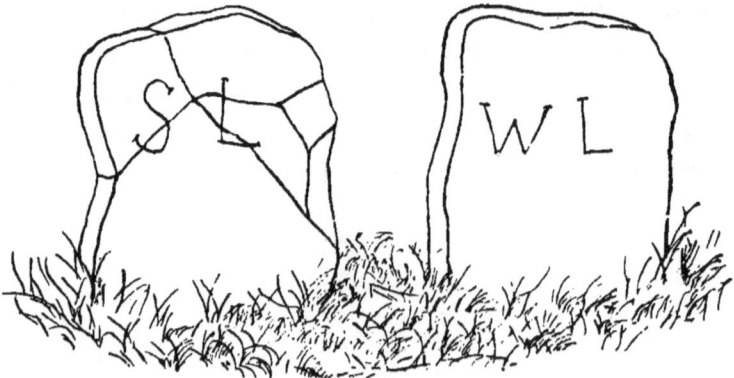

www.ingramcontent.com/pod-product-compliance
Lightning Source LLC
Chambersburg PA
CBHW021632270326
41931CB00008B/984